Teach

Math

Tables

To

Your

Kid

[ZHINGOORA BOOKS]

Digits

51 - Fifty One

52 - Fifty Two

53 - Fifty Three

54 - Fifty Four

55 - Fifty Five

56 - Fifty Six

57 - Fifty Seven

58 - Fifty Eight

59 - Fifty Nine

60 - Sixty

51 Times Table

51 x 1 = 51

51 x 2 = 102

51 x 3 = 153

51 x 4 = 204

51 x 5 = 255

51 x 6 = 306

51 x 7 = 357

51 x 8 = 408

51 x 9 = 459

51 x 10 = 510

52 Times Table

52 x 1 = 52

52 x 2 = 104

52 x 3 = 156

52 x 4 = 208

52 x 5 = 260

52 x 6 = 312

52 x 7 = 364

52 x 8 = 416

52 x 9 = 468

52 x 10 = 520

53 Times Table

53 x 1 = 53

53 x 2 = 106

53 x 3 = 159

53 x 4 = 212

53 x 5 = 265

53 x 6 = 318

53 x 7 = 371

53 x 8 = 424

53 x 9 = 477

53 x 10 = 530

54 Times Table

54 x 1 = 54

54 x 2 = 108

54 x 3 = 162

54 x 4 = 216

54 x 5 = 270

54 x 6 = 324

54 x 7 = 378

54 x 8 = 432

54 x 9 = 486

54 x 10 = 540

55 Times Table

55 x 1 = 55

55 x 2 = 110

55 x 3 = 165

55 x 4 = 220

55 x 5 = 275

55 x 6 = 330

55 x 7 = 385

55 x 8 = 440

55 x 9 = 495

55 x 10 = 550

56 Times Table

56 x 1 = 56

56 x 2 = 112

56 x 3 = 168

56 x 4 = 224

56 x 5 = 280

56 x 6 = 336

56 x 7 = 392

56 x 8 = 448

56 x 9 = 504

56 x 10 = 560

57 Times Table

57 x 1 = 57

57 x 2 = 114

57 x 3 = 171

57 x 4 = 228

57 x 5 = 285

57 x 6 = 342

57 x 7 = 399

57 x 8 = 456

57 x 9 = 513

57 x 10 = 570

58 Times Table

58 x 1 = 58

58 x 2 = 116

58 x 3 = 174

58 x 4 = 232

58 x 5 = 290

58 x 6 = 348

58 x 7 = 406

58 x 8 = 464

58 x 9 = 522

58 x 10 = 580

59 Times Table

59 x 1 = 59

59 x 2 = 118

59 x 3 = 177

59 x 4 = 236

59 x 5 = 295

59 x 6 = 354

59 x 7 = 413

59 x 8 = 472

59 x 9 = 531

59 x 10 = 590

60 Times Table

60 x 1 = 60

60 x 2 = 120

60 x 3 = 180

60 x 4 = 240

60 x 5 = 300

60 x 6 = 360

60 x 7 = 420

60 x 8 = 480

60 x 9 = 540

60 x 10 = 600

End of the book.

www.ingramcontent.com/pod-product-compliance
Lightning Source LLC
Chambersburg PA
CBHW060023300526
45794CB00003B/1274